Mc

• BOOK 2 •

A
*Woman's*
*Stand!*

Marilyn S. Braxton

Published in Ashburn, Virginia, by
Braxton Press Productions, www.braxtonpress.com

ISBN 978-0-9978372-0-9

Printed in the United States of America

# Contents

# A
# *Woman's Stand!*

Marilyn S. Braxton

# *Foreword*

As Christians, we always hear the word, "Faith," throughout the Bible, from a pastor, from family, from friends, and even proclaiming it to ourselves.

There comes a time when we really <u>have to put the word, "Faith," to test ourselves</u> when our loved ones are in serious illness, even to the point of death. We don't want it to happen to our loved ones, but no one knows tomorrow except for God. We do have some control in life, but at times, we don't.

As Christians, we need to have "Faith" when we are faced with challenges because Jesus Christ has won the victory. In him, we are fulfilled; therefore we can put "Faith" to work with the Word of God and go to it with a focused passion.

This is what my sister, Marilyn, had to do. Her main focus was using the Word of God and combining it with "Faith," to get the result she needed for her husband, Dean.

Dean being healed was the destination of her focus. She wore the Armor of God (Eph. 6:12-17) and went to battle with the devil with her non-stop prayers, her family, and the body of Christ. She had the mindset that she was unstoppable!

The process was not an easy one, and it wasn't a choice Marilyn had settled in her mind to finish this chapter of her life and put the Word of God to work. The Word is Truth. The Word will work, if you work along with it.

Marilyn prayed and proclaimed Dean healed. She called things that were not as though they were (Romans 4:17). When he received his healing, all she could do was to thank and praise God. By the way, Marilyn is my prayer partner.

I Love you always, Sis.
—Mi-Sun Haymond

# Introduction

I praise and honor God for the favor He has shown the Braxton family.

In the Bible, God gives us accounts of women of great faith. We are blessed to live in the twenty-first century with women who continue to manifest great faith. I am blessed to be able to bear witness to such a woman, my daughter-in-law, Marilyn Braxton.

My husband and I flew to Tacoma, Washington, on May 6, 2006. Marilyn had put on the full armor of God (Ephesians 6:10-18) during my son's illness and revival from death.

Because of her faith, her obedience to God, and her full armor stance, I am so grateful to God for allowing her to go boldly before the throne in prayer to ask for the healing of her husband, my son, Dean Braxton. Mother's Day, Sunday, May 14, 2006, Dean was transferred from Tacoma General Hospital's Intensive Care Unit (ICU) to a

6th floor room where Marilyn led us in prayer. I shall always be grateful to God and my daughter-in-law, a woman of strong faith, for the precious gift of another Mother's Day spent with my son here on earth.

All praises to God for using Marilyn as a blessing to our son and the Braxton family.

As the song goes, "To God Be the Glory For the things He has done."

—Mrs. Freddie Mae Braxton,
A grateful Mother-in-law

# My Wife

## By Dean A. Braxton

This book is about a battle my wife had to fight for my life on this earth. She did something that many of us would like to do. She trusted, put her faith into practice through the power of God that brought a person back from death to life, but also I was totally healed of any physical problems. The whole story is in the book called *In Heaven! Experiencing the Throne of God.* This little book was taken out of that book to read so others can see what it took her to get what she wanted, the life and healing of me, her husband.

I saw ten things within the story that she did to see the power of God move in a way that she needed to see me alive back on earth. They are: **1:** She first reached out to those she believed would stop and pray. **2:** In the midst of the storm, she praised God. **3:** She had a close walk with God before this incident had happened. **4:** She kept her mind on what the Bible said. **5:** She was acting on what she had read Paul had done in the Bible. **6:** She protected her husband from negative people and prayers. **7:** She was in this battle to win and no matter what godly sacrifices it took. **8:** She took control of her thinking and kept it on God's promises. **9:** She kept pressing in to God and relying on His strength. **10:** She knew whose power and strength was helping her through.

Within these next few pages you will read what it took for her to get what she wanted within God's will. She knew that it was not God's will that I die May 5, 2006; she knew God had a plan still for me on this earth that we are currently fulfilling. So as you read on, know that you can have the same results in anything you believe for, that is within God's will. As you read *A Woman's Stand!* we pray you come to know how the power of God's word acted on can truly work in this world today.

# A Woman's Stand!

## *Marilyn's Testimony*

**Thursday, May 4th**—"I discovered that Dean was in the St. Francis Hospital Emergency Room at 12 noon after checking my voice mail. There was a message from one of the nurses telling me I needed to pick Dean up and take him home. I was working at another hospital and told the nurse I needed to leave.

"When I got to the hospital, Dean was asleep from the pain medication they had given him. The Emergency Room doctor then told me that Dean had kidney stones and a kidney infection with one of the stones located high up on his right side, which was the one that was causing Dean the most pain. The doctor suggested Dean stay overnight to get IV antibiotics and fluids. Dean was in-and-out of the conversation due to the sedation caused by the pain medication.

"Later that evening, a Urologist (kidney specialist) came in to see Dean. He told us that it would be a good idea to have the stones blasted by ultra sound on Friday morning and Dean would not have to endure all that pain. We agreed, knowing Dean would be home the next day. When I left the hospital, Dean was having chills and a fever, but sleeping in intervals."

**Friday Morning, May 5th**—"Dean is still out of it, due to the medication and a temperature of 104, but still went into surgery. When we went into the surgery waiting area to answer questions, Dean asked at one point if the process was over when he had not even gone into the operating room.

"After the surgery, Dean was in recovery for almost three hours. I spent the last half hour with him in recovery. While we waited, the doctor who had administered Dean's pain medicine while he was in surgery came and told me Dean had a very bad infection and needed to go to Intense Care Unit (ICU) to receive fluids, more antibiotics, and to be observed. I talked to my husband while in recovery. He was complaining about the oxygen mask being uncomfortable, and the nurses changed it for him. Dean was attached to different IV pumps in his arm. When we got to the room in ICU, I only talked to my husband briefly when the ICU doctor told us they wanted to put a pic-line in Dean's neck so they could take away some of the lines in his arm, and if so, a pic-line would be easy if they needed to draw blood for tests. Dean understood that this was going to happen as I then left for them to start the procedure.

"The nurse came into the waiting area to get me, but when I got to the room, the pic-line was already in Dean's chest. I looked at my husband and could see he was hardly breathing and his lips looked ashy or gray. I asked what happened and the doctor told me they reached a blockage in Dean's neck. I was told immediately they needed to intubate (put a tube down Dean's throat) or else he could die, and there was not time to think about it.

"At that time we lived 5 minutes from the hospital and I left as they were doing this procedure to pick up some things (of course praying on the way). As I drove onto the street, the surgeon called me on my cell phone to tell me my husband coded (his heart stopped) and they were doing CPR (Cardiopulmonary Resuscitation). All I could say was, "What?"

"I called our son and daughter, Gabriel and Tiffany, who were away at college, to tell them to pray for their dad. I continued home praying more intensely, and calling others asking them to pray also. I called a friend who was on her way to the hospital and she said she would come by to pick me up.

"When we got there, we did not see Dean right away for they were still working with him. Of course, I got in touch with Dean's parents. They had been visiting relatives in Texas and had to return to California prior to coming to Washington. They talked with the doctor and came as fast as they could. The doctors worked on Dean for 1 hour and 45 minutes. It was during this time, friends showed up in the waiting area and we prayed together in faith for Dean. After we prayed, I felt compelled to sing a song of praise and glorify the Lord."

"The doctor came and told me how touch-and-go things were, and they would know more by morning. Dean was being prayed for in many places throughout the world. We did not demand God in prayer, we did not beg Him, but we asked the Father in Jesus name. We thanked the Lord God that Dean was healed by the stripes of Jesus. I refused to doubt, but trusted the Word of God for His promise concerning Dean's life.

"I knew I had access to the throne of grace and that I could go boldly as a child of the Most High. Not only did I ask, but also I thanked the Lord for what He was doing in Dean even though the circumstances looked bad. I purposed in my heart not to blame God, for it is the devil that comes to steal, kill, and destroy. Jesus comes to give abundant life (John 10:10) and I claimed that life for my husband."

## John 10:10 (NKJV)

*The thief does not come except to steal, and to kill, and to destroy. I (Jesus) have come that they may have life, and that they may have it more abundantly.*

"It was all so crazy and so sudden. Before I left the hospital, Dean's body was already filling up with the fluids they were putting in him. I felt the need to go home and battle the enemy, for I did not know what the rest of the night would bring Dean. A friend stayed overnight with her son. Before the night was over, Dean was on several medications, including insulin.

"When I arrived home, I cried. I thanked the Lord for what a good husband Dean has been (he put up with me). I thanked the Lord for him being a good father to our children. I released the angels of God to be encamped roundabout Dean. I did not get much sleep that night and found myself on the floor the next morning, as I would do the next three mornings praying in the spirit. I still believe there is power in the shed blood of Jesus and I covered Dean in that blood.

**Saturday Morning, May 6th**—"Dean's blood sugar was 500 and I was told that he needed to be transferred to a different hospital, Tacoma General, to be on Kidney Dialysis continually, because his kidneys did not function at all during the night and his body was going into septic shock. Dean's body was very large from the fluids. He was on 100% ventilation (the machine was doing the breathing for him). Dean went by ambulance that day with a nurse to care for the pumps, the breathing tube, and to suction him if needed.

"I could see that even through this relocation the Lord caused Dean to be transferred to a hospital they normally would not have sent him to. Later on, I had been talking to the supervisor of nurses that was in charge that day. I knew her since I had worked at this hospital before. She was very surprised that Dean was my husband and was very glad that she had chosen to take him at Tacoma General Hospital.

"Most of the time a patient coming from St. Francis in Federal Way would go to their bigger local sister hospital, which should have been St. Joseph Hospital in Tacoma. She said when she got the call that day to take this crucial ill patient from St. Francis Hospital she knew she should. So as the nursing supervisor she accepted Dean as a patient and when asked by the charge nurse why she was doing it, she said, "I did not know, but I felt that we should." The Lord is good!

"Dean had a very good nurse on duty that morning at the hospital he had been transferred to. The nurse was very positive and I knew that we would get along just fine. Dean was hooked up to dialysis right away. He just laid there without a clue of what was going on. Many came to pray for him and many made themselves available to me if I needed anything. I refused to accept a negative report. I did not deny there were negative reports, I just refused to accept them, and refused to let those reports be the final answer. One doctor told me it could be a long time before Dean would be back to himself, and there could be a possibility of brain damage. I then told him that it did not have to be a long time."

"When I got home that night, I prayed for Dean long, hard and loud. I told the devil who comes to steal, kill and destroy to take his hands off my husband. My body felt as if it was on fire as sweat dripped onto my nightshirt. It got so wet I took it off laid it on a chair. I took the shirt with me the next morning to the hospital and laid it on Dean's head."

## Acts 19:11-12 (NKJV)

*Now God worked unusual miracles by the hands of Paul, so that even handkerchiefs or aprons were brought from his body to the sick, and the diseases left them and the evil spirits went out of them.*

"Tiffany and Gabriel were in constant prayer themselves, and had put their dad on a prayer chain with several of their friends in school.

"I did not want anything negative spoken over my husband or to him, nor did I want any negative or hopeless prayers prayed. I remember saying to the Father, "I curse every negative word and prayer spoken over or to my husband in the name of Jesus!" I really did not want anyone going in, feeling sorry for Dean, or to think that there was no hope. Death and life are in the power of the tongue, and I made sure my tongue spoke life, for THE WORD OF GOD IS LIFE! I did not have time to feel sorry for Dean and I made no time to feel sorry for him. I felt I was in a battle and I wanted to win."

## PROVERBS 18:21 (NKJV)

*Death and life are in the power of the tongue,*
*And those who love it will eat its fruit*

**Sunday, May 7th**—"The Word of God was preached to some of us in the waiting area and we sang praises. We were still not giving up on Dean. My daughter phoned me and told me to read Psalms 40. My son was calling everyday to talk to the doctor or nurse about his dad's condition. There was a time when the thought came to my mind, "get the funeral ready." Immediately, I brought my thoughts into captivity to the obedience of Christ and I told the devil he was and is a liar. I continued to thank God for His promise in Psalms 103:3, for forgiving all Dean's iniquities, and healing all of Dean's diseases."

## PSALM 103:3 (NKJV)

*Who forgives all your iniquities, Who heals*
*all your diseases*

"GLORY! Dean did respond this day but does not remember. Dean opened his eyes and looked around as to say, what is going on? I told him I loved him as also one

21

of our friends who was with me. The nurse did not want him to get to excited, and so increased the sedative and put him back to sleep."

**Monday, May 8th**—"Dean's parents are here. Praise God! For the next few days my mother-in-law and I sang to Dean, read James 5:13-15, and anointed him with oil."

---

### James 5:13-15 (NKJV)

*Is anyone among you suffering? Let him pray. Is anyone cheerful? Let him sing psalms. Is anyone among you sick? Let him call for the elders of the church, and let them pray over him, anointing him with oil in the name of the Lord. And the prayer of faith will save the sick, and the Lord will raise him up. And if he has committed sins, he will be forgiven.*

---

"Sometimes Dean's father would go somewhere else to say his prayers.

"I was tired in the body, but my spirit was strong. I was so tired one night, when I arrived at the house, I turned the car off, put my head back and fell fast asleep. When I awoke, I went into the house and prayed. All this happened so fast and unexpectedly. How could something so minor turn out to be so major, so suddenly? I continued to press in closer to the Lord."

"During the past days the doctors would see Dean improve and then slip back to where he had been before. One day he would have a temperature, and they would take him to get a CAT scan to see if the infection had spread. Then the test would come back negative. His white blood count would go up and the potassium would be low. One day he would be down 50% on the ventilator, and that evening it might go back up. I was still trusting God. Dean was on six different medications and most was for his blood pressure, of which one of the medicines was detrimental to Dean's health, I was told by the doctors.

"One of our friends prayed for Dean with such compassion that he kissed Dean's feet as he was praying, he had no idea of the condition my husband's feet were in. Dean's toes were purple and black from the medicine and he had lost feeling in them. We found out later, the doctors were planning on cutting his toes off. Dean also had a feeding tube in for a couple of days toward the end of his stay in ICU."

**Tuesday, May 9th**—"Dean's healing was taking place fast. It surprised the doctors and nurses and other staff who knew of his case. One doctor would say, he is getting better but we still need to take it slow. Another doctor would say, "Wow he's improved 200-300% in such a short time."

"Many things still happened as Dean's body was healing. The nurse was extremely happy when Dean could follow commands and told the doctor the next day that he was still following commands and that Dean had not skipped a beat. The night of May 9th, I came home and purposed in my heart that I would spend all night in prayer for Dean and found out the next day that a friend said he was tired of the situation and that he would be in prayer all night."

**Wednesday Morning May 10th**—"Five young boys from High School showed up to pray for Dean during school hours. These boys touched the heart of the nurse that morning and he said he would never forget the prayer and love, and the presence he felt in the room.

"This day he was also taken off the ventilator and dialysis. The nurses asked Dean if he was in any pain, and he shook his head no. They also explained the procedure for removing the breathing tube, and that another breathing treatment would have to be given a half hour later to make sure he could stay off the ventilator.

"The nurses told my in-laws and I to take a long lunch break. Prior to leaving for lunch I spoke in Dean's ear and said to him, "breath for me, breath for your children and breath for your friends, BREATH"! He shook his head yes. Dean had a puzzled look on his face, as to say, "What happened?" Dean had this look before but was unable to speak because of the tube. By this time, Dean was down to taking 1-2 medications.

"Praise God! Psalms 68:35 was one of the scriptures I held on to, for I needed God's strength and His power."

### PSALM 68:35 (NKJV)

*O God, You are more awesome than Your holy places. The God of Israel is He who gives strength and power to His people. Blessed be God!*

"Upon returning to the hospital after a great lunch with one of our friends, it was awesome to see Dean sitting up in bed. It was good to hear his voice again. It was a great celebration. Many of the nurses who did not have Dean as a patient came to celebrate his recovery. The nurses were glad to see someone who had made it through all of this, also because it was Nurse's Week and they needed to have a happy ending themselves.

"Other staff came as well to see the progress Dean had made, the only word used was, "Miracle", and boy did we know that! Some came even a couple of days later and they were calling him the miracle man. The fluid was leaving Dean's body and his kidneys were working fine.

"Then Dean asked the big question, "Would you please sit down and tell me what happened to me?" When I told him, he cried and of course, I told him more than once. He wanted to know every detail. It really touched him to know so many cared and prayed; many that we had never met before and some we have yet to meet. Dean was able to get up for about 15 minutes in a chair. This was the first night I stayed with him. I was his nurse that night."

**May 14th, Mother's Day**—"Dean was moved to another floor. He walked down the long hall to the family visiting room. Dean could not feel his toes, for they were numb. The doctors were still in awe of the miracle that had taken place before their eyes. Dean spent 13 days in the hospital, and 9 of those days were in ICU.

*"The effective, fervent* (red-hot) *prayer of a righteous man avails much* (James 5:16). We do give God Almighty all the glory for He is faithful to His word."

**May 16th**—"Dean came home, where he stayed for one and a half months. When Dean returned to work, he worked half days for 5 weeks. Dean's toes are completely healed. He is not taking any medications. After the 5 weeks, he was back working full time. Dean has had several check-ups and tests since he has been home and the doctors had given him a clean bill of health. One doctor told Dean he should tell the story of the miracle that he is alive. Another doctor told Dean, "a lot of people prayed hard for you." Another doctor said, "I was so scared, I have not been that scared in a long time because things happened so fast."

"Dean has been back to the hospital to visit and they are still saying what a miracle it is. They had him come one day to rounds, so that others on staff could see him.

"Later we found out that when the doctor blasted the stones, the poisons from the infection got into his bloodstream and all of his entire vital organs had shut down. One nurse told us later that we have bad outcomes with these cases.

"Psalm 14:1 says, *The fool has said in his heart, "There is no God."* Well, there is a God, He is alive, and miracles do happen. He is the Great Jehovah, God Almighty, Lord of Lords and King of Kings! I bless the readers of this testimony in Jesus name. My prayer for you is that you would take up your cross and follow Jesus daily, and that you would walk a life pleasing to Him. That He would become the lover of your soul as He is mine, in Jesus name."

—Marilyn Braxton

# Pressing In

*The Devil is a liar*
*He is not your friend*
*When he knocks at your door*
*Start Pressing In*
*He hits below the waist*
*And will fight you to the end*
*It's an attack on your faith*
*Start Pressing In*
*He comes to kill, steal, and destroy*
*Fighting you tooth and nail*
*Stand firmly on the Word*
*Start Pressing in*
*Go boldly to the throne*
*Making your request known*
*Putting on the full armor of God*
*Start Pressing In*
*Breastplate of righteousness*

*The shield of faith*
*Helmet of salvation*
*Sword of the Spirit*
*And your feet shod with the preparation*
*Of the Gospel Peace*
*Dress from head to toe*
*You won't bend, bow, or break*
*The righteous always prevail*
*Make no mistake*
*The devil doesn't quit*
*He will knock again*
*Pretending to be your friend*
*Stand firm and believe God's Word*
*Remember the promises He made to you*
*Where you Press In*
*He Presses With You*

by
Dorothea Holmess

# Afterword
# by Dean A. Braxton

Before this incident took place, I was a very healthy 47-year-old male. I had regular physical checkups. Most of these checkups were because I was in the United States Air Force on active duty for 6 years and reserve duty for 14 years. I retired from the Reserves with a clean bill of health. The only problem that I had after that was kidney stones in June of 2002, four years prior to this incident.

I went through the same procedure back then for kidney stones as I did for this incident. The biggest difference was staying in the hospital overnight before the operation. In June of 2002, I checked into the hospital that morning and came out in the afternoon of the same day.

The following is taken from the Medical Records we received from both hospitals that I was admitted into. Now, to get these records was not easy, because of the mistakes that were made and the potential of a lawsuit.

The doctor who made the mistakes made it hard for us to receive accurate reports. Finally, we had to get other doctors who worked on my case to give us the information.

It has never been our intention to sue the doctor or the hospital. We just wanted the official medical records to support the medical testimonies we had received from doctors, nurses, and other people who worked in the hospitals.

The other thing about these records is that it has been hard to get a medical professional to read what we have and write it down for this book. We came up against resistance from people not wanting to go on record in translating the medical account. They just did not want to support in writing the number of mistakes that were made by the Urologist and hospital. Again, they did not want to be a part of any potential lawsuit in the future. So, the following is raw information that will have to be translated by the reader.

During the next four years after the first treatment for kidney stones, I did not have any problems with kidney stones or any other illness. I do not remember taking any sick leave for personal illness.

# Excerpts of Information Taken From My Medical Records and Medical Transcripts

**Preoperative Diagnosis:** Left ureteral calculus and bilateral nephrolithiasis (kidney stones) and pyelonephritis (urinary tract infection)

**Postoperative Diagnosis:** Left ureteral calculus and bilateral nephrolithiasis and pyelonephritis

**Operation:** Cystoscopy with retrograde pyelogram, push back of ureteral calculus and bilateral extracorporeal shock wave lithotripsy

**Indications:** This delightful 49-year-old gentleman *(really 47-year-old)* presented to the hospital with pyelonephritis and obstruction ureteral calculus. After 24 hours of antibiotic coverage with supplemental antibiotic administration in operation room, he presents at this time for definitive surgical intervention.

**Findings:** Obstructing calculus in the left ureter is pushed back in the renal pelvis, and a 24-cm 7-french double-J stent is left in place in the ureter and that calculus further targets and both kidneys were fragmented with difficulty.

After 2400 shocks, the procedure was terminated and the patient was awakened and returned to the recovery room in satisfactory condition. There were no complications. He tolerated the procedure well.

> *—This was from a May 6, 2006, report by the surgeon who performed the original operation.*

# Excerpts Taken From the Rest of the Medical Records and Medical Transcripts

- Larger amount of fluid resuscitation for hypertension
- Poorly responsive
- Move legs to pain
- Very cool digits with cyanotic toes
- Acute renal failure
- Secondary to acute tubular necrosis oliguric
- Profound septic shock
- Prolonged Cardiac Arrest
- CPR 1 hour and 45 minutes
- Septic shock with urasepisis
- Respiratory failure
- Pulmonary infiltrates
- Edema versus adult respiratory distress Syndrome
- Post prolonged CPR
- Post cardiac arrest

- Prolonged resuscitation
- Fulminant sepsis
- Too numerous to count stone in right kidney
- Chest x-rays show the development of diffuse pulmonary edema
- Urine culture sent yesterday is growing greater than 100,000 colonies of E. coli.
- Doctor reports of spent a total of 1 hour and 45 min. total critical care time with the patient not including procedure
- Servere sepsis
- Diagnosis of SIRS/Sepsis with hypotension, tachycardia, tachypnea, hypoxemia.
- High risk of disseminated intravascular coagulation.
- Cardiac arrest
- Urasepsis with E. coli.
- Secondary renal shut down.
- Asystable
- Extubated
- Herodynamically Stable
- Shock liver
- Shock syndrome
- Hemodynamic stress
- On mechanical ventilation

- Paralytic ileus
- Multi-organ failure
- Critically ill
- Prognosis is poor
- Quniton Cathetar and dialysis treatment (risk & Benefits)
- Risk for bleeding complication with ongoing DIC
- Clotting dialysis system given ongoing DIC
- Obstruction urinary stones
- Severely acidotic with a lactic acid as high as 16.
- Poorly responsive
- Requiring High Fio Moderate to severe patchy air space
- Opacities in the lungs bilaterally slightly increased. This is ward son for progression of pneumonia.
- Very unfortunate critically ill patient.

After the recovery, I did receive some resistance from the doctor who had performed the operation in taking out a stent that was placed in my body. My wife had to call the doctor and state that she was going to take legal action if we did not receive an appointment to have the stent removed. We did receive an appointment for the next day, and the doctor removed the stent.

I asked him at that time what happened to cause my heart to stop. He said that I had a bad infection that he thought was taken care of with some real strong medicine. But for some reason the infection was not affected by the medicine that had been given to me. He said they had not checked prior to the operation to see if the medicine worked or not, and they had just assumed it did. It was not until five days later, that they found out from lab reports that the medicine did not have any effect on the infection.

At the time of the incident, the doctor did not know what was going wrong or why my vital organs were shutting down. The doctor told me that if they would not have done everything right, I would have been behind the eight ball (dead). If they would have done a process ten minutes earlier or ten minutes later, I would have been behind the eight ball.

I did ask him if I had died. He said my heart had stopped and that every time it looked like it was going to start, it would not. He said they worked on me about 1 hour and 30 minutes (Official record stated 1 hour and 45 minutes). I asked him if he saw this as a miracle, and he said it was and that I should go tell the story.

As you can read there were a lot of things that just went wrong with the procedures and my body. Thank God for Marilyn taking a Stand.

*Finally, my brethren, be strong in the Lord and in the power of His might. Put on the whole armor of God, that you may be able to stand against the wiles of the devil. For we do not wrestle against flesh and blood, but against principalities, against powers, against the rulers of the darkness of this age, against spiritual hosts of wickedness in the heavenly places. Therefore take up the whole armor of God, that you may be able to withstand in the evil day, and having done all, to stand. Stand therefore, having girded your waist with truth, having put on the breastplate of righteousness, and having shod your feet with the preparation of the gospel of peace; above all, taking the shield of faith with which you will be able to quench all the fiery darts of the wicked one. And take the helmet of salvation, and the sword of the Spirit, which is the word of God; praying always with all prayer and supplication in the Spirit, being watchful to this end with all perseverance and supplication for all the saints—and for me, that utterance may be given to me, that I may open my mouth boldly to make known the mystery of the gospel, for which I am an ambassador in chains; that in it I may speak boldly, as I ought to speak.*

Made in the USA
Middletown, DE
10 October 2025